A Merry-Mouse
Christmas A·B·C

MERRY-MOUSE BOOK™

A Merry-Mouse Christmas A·B·C

by Priscilla Hillman

Doubleday & Company, Inc., Garden City, New York

Library of Congress Cataloging in Publication Data

Hillman, Priscilla.
A merry-mouse Christmas A B C.

SUMMARY: Verses introduce the ABC's of Christmas
such as angel, berries, and candle.
1. Alphabet rhymes.   [1. Christmas poetry.
2. Alphabet]   I. Title.
PZ8.3.H5544Me   811'.5'4

Library of Congress Catalog Card Number 79-6586

ISBN: 0-385-15596-4 Trade
ISBN: 0-385-15597-2 Prebound
Copyright © 1980 by Priscilla Hillman
All Rights Reserved
Printed in the United States of America
9 8 7 6 5 4 3

To Norm, my husband

$\mathcal{A}$ is for angel
dressed up in white,
with wings and a halo
so shiny and bright.

B is for berries
I'll take home with me
to bake in a pie
or string for the tree.

C is for candle
that sheds a soft light
and makes things seem cozy
on a cold, snowy night.

D is for drum
being played by a mouse,
going rat-a-tat-tat
all through the house.

$\mathcal{E}$ is for evergreen
branches of pine
we pick for the mantelpiece.
Won't they look fine?

F is for fireside
all warm and glowing,
while outside the window
a cold wind is blowing.

G is for gingerbread
so spicy and sweet.
This gingerbread man
looks too good to eat.

H is for holly
to deck through the house,
being gathered for Christmas
by one little mouse.

I is for ice skates
found under the tree.
We'll try them together.
Hold on to me!

J is for jingle bells
all shiny and bright.
We're getting them ready
for a sleighride tonight.

K is for kisses
under mistletoe balls,
while giggles and laughter
are heard through the halls.

L is for letters
to jolly St. Nick;
Scritch-scratch goes the pen;
must get this out quick.

$\mathcal{M}$ is for Merry Christmas,
the greeting we hear
when it's time to build snowmice
and spread Christmas cheer.

N is for nuts,
a very good treat;
the nut cracker cracks,
but the mice get to eat.

O is for ornament.
Ooops! This one broke.
It looked bright and pretty
'til I gave it a poke.

P is for presents
all done up in bows.
But what is inside them?
Nobody knows.

Q is for quiet
all through the house,
not a creature was stirring,
not even a mouse.

$\mathcal{R}$ is for Rudolph,
whose nose is so red,
and eight other reindeer
who pull Santa's sled.

S is for stockings
all hung in a row
waiting for Santa
to stuff to the toe.

T is for tree
trimmed the old-fashioned way
with berries and popcorn
before Christmas day.

U is for uniform
on a soldier of wood;
the mice wished to play,
but the toy only stood.

V is for visions
of sugarplums sweet,
of candy canes, mints,
and good things to eat.

W is for wreath
made of pine boughs and holly.
My snowman and I
think it looks very jolly.

X is for Xmas,
that wonderful day.
My stocking is full,
and I feel warm and gay.

Y is for Yule log
being dragged through the woods
by two little mice
wearing mittens and hoods.

Z is for z
on the alphabet block.
Midnight is sounding
on the grandfather clock.

We hope you're all snug
in your beds sleeping tight,
for Santa Claus wishes you
all a good night.